Golden Pheasant

Scarlet Macaw

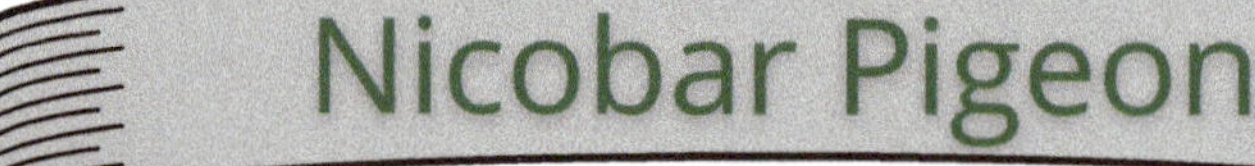

Nicobar Pigeon

Flamingo

Mandarin Duck

Red-necked Tanager

Blue Jay

Peacock

Blue Crowned Pigeon

Keel-billed Toucan

Red Crested Turaco

Hyacinth Macaw

Painted Bunting

Atlantic Puffin

Wood duck

Gouldian Finch

Purple Gallinule

Rainbow Lorikeet

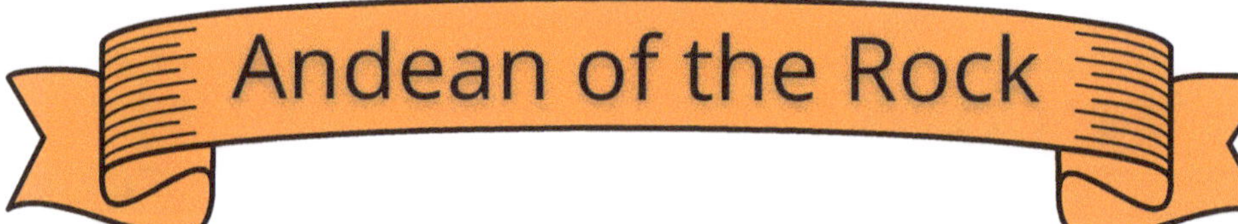

Andean of the Rock

Dwarf kingfisher

Bearded Reedling

Hooded Pitta

Magpie

Yellow Oriole

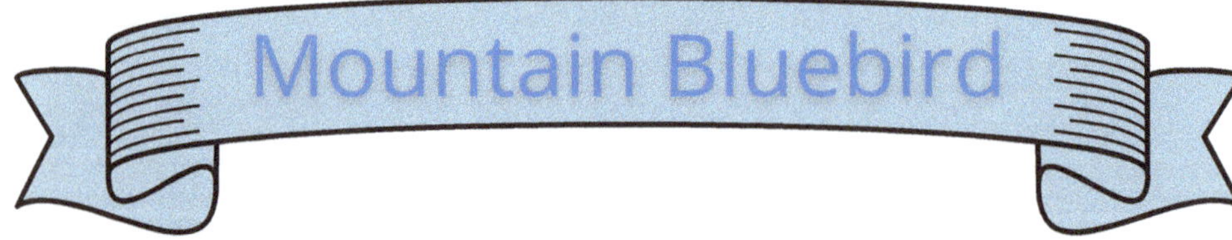

Mountain Bluebird

Blue Tit

Pink Galah

Goldcrest

Hoopoe

Collared Lory

Paradise Flycatcher

Redwing Blackbird

Tilhi

Quetzal

Ruby Topaz Hummingbird

Pink Robin

Scaly-Breasted Munia

Indian Roller

Inca Tern

Crested Duck

Waved Albatross

Rufous-Crested Coquette

Great Hornbill

Kookaburra

Fairy Wren

Sea Eagle

Emperor Penguin

Dalmatian Pelican

Snow Goose

Hoatzin

Secretary Bird

Ross's Gull

Snowy Owl

Snow Petrel

Eurasian Skylark

Common Eider

Hypocolius

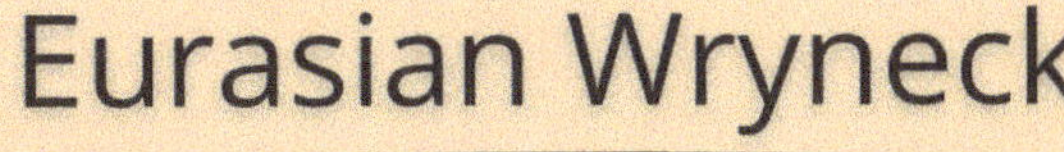

Eurasian Wryneck

Egyptian Plover

Montagu's Harrier